Delicious
pastries

Delicious pastries

Love Food ™ is an imprint of Parragon Books Ltd

Parragon
Queen Street House
4 Queen Street
Bath BA1 1HE, UK

Copyright © Parragon Books Ltd 2007

Love Food ™ and the accompanying heart device is a trademark of Parragon Books Ltd.

Cover and internal design by Mark Cavanagh
Introduction by Bridget Jones
Photography by Günter Beer
Additional photography by Mike Cooper
Home Economist Stevan Paul

ISBN 978-1-4054-9271-3
Printed in China

Notes for the reader
• This book uses imperial, metric, and US cup measurements. Follow the same units of measurement throughout; do not mix imperial and metric.
• All spoon measurements are level: teaspoons are assumed to be 5 ml, and tablespoons are assumed to be 15 ml.
• Unless otherwise stated, milk is assumed to be lowfat and eggs are medium. The times given are an approximate guide only.
• Some recipes contain nuts. If you are allergic to nuts you should avoid using them and any products containing nuts. Recipes using raw or very lightly cooked eggs should be avoided by infants, the elderly, pregnant women, convalescents, and anyone suffering from illness.

Contents

Pastries

Pastry chef superiority should not deter anyone from trying basic pastry-making methods. Getting it right is no mystery, but a matter of a few general guidelines with the right technique for the right dough.
• Cool ingredients, hands, equipment, and environment suit pastry making.
• Allow chilling time when necessary—it makes the difference between unmanageable dough and roll-easy results.
• Practice a light touch to avoid tough dough. Use fingertips, not palms, to rub fat into flour. A food processor is great for rubbing fat into flour and kneading Danish dough.
• There is no need to grease pans unless the recipe specifically advises you to do so.
• Most pastries benefit from being baked at high temperatures, at least at first.

Fantastic filo
Purchase filo from a store with a good turnover (old stock tends to be brittle).
• Cover filo with clear film or a damp dish towel when not actually handling it, as the sheets dry quickly to become brittle.
• Brush filo with fat to make the edges adhere and to keep the layers crisp and separate. A little oil works but melted butter is traditional; a mix of butter melted in oil works well too.

Perfect puff and Danish pastries
Keeping everything well chilled is vital for success. Chill between rolling the layers, allowing time for the dough to rest. Danish, in particular, has to be left overnight before finally rolling out and shaping.
• Bake puff pastry at a high temperature for the layers to rise and separate.

• Rinse baking pans in cold water, or put a roasting pan of boiling water in the bottom of the oven, to give a good rise.

• Brush puff and Danish with egg or milk to glaze; egg white and sugar make a sweet glaze for sweet pastries.

Simply choux

Choux pastry is so simple to make; it is just a case of using the right method at the right time.

• Melt the butter in the water slowly, without boiling until the fat has melted, then bring to a boil quickly.

• Add the flour (always all-purpose) in one go before removing the pan from the heat and stirring immediately. Stir until the mixture comes away from the pan but do not beat or it will become greasy.

• Leave the paste to cool slightly before adding the eggs.

• Beat in the eggs. An electric beater is useful for this. Continue beating until the mixture is smooth and glossy.

• Split cooked choux pastries immediately after removing them from the oven to allow the steam to escape and keep the outside crisp; the inside should be slightly sticky.

So short

Short pastries are crumbly and crisp, held together by fat and flour with a little liquid. Too much water will make the dough tough, as will heavy handling.

• A high proportion of fat makes rich, very short pastry—the usual amount is half fat to flour, or three-quarters fat to flour for rich, short pastries.

• Butter gives the best flavor; shortening makes the mixture very short. The classic combination is half and half of each.

1

Perfect Puff

apple danish

makes 16

for the Danish pastry dough

2½ cups white bread flour, plus extra for dusting

¾ cup butter, well chilled, plus extra for greasing

¼ tsp salt

¼ oz/7 g active dry yeast

2 tbsp superfine sugar

1 egg, at room temperature

1 tsp vanilla extract

6 tbsp lukewarm water

milk, for glazing

for the filling

2 baking apples, peeled, cored, and chopped

grated rind of 1 lemon

4 tbsp sugar

Place the flour in a bowl and rub in 2 tablespoons of the butter. Set aside. Chill the remaining butter in the freezer until hard but not frozen. Dust with flour and grate coarsely into a bowl. Chill.

Stir the salt, yeast, and sugar into the flour mixture. In another bowl, beat the egg with the vanilla extract and water, then add to the flour and mix to form a dough. Knead the dough for 10 minutes on a floured surface, then chill for 10 minutes.

Roll out the dough to 12 x 8 inches/30 x 20 cm and mark it lengthwise into thirds. Sprinkle the grated butter evenly over the top two-thirds, leaving a ½–¾-inch/1–2-cm border around the edge, and press down lightly.

Fold the bottom third of dough over the center, then fold the top third down. Press the edges of the dough with a rolling pin and give it a quarter-turn (so the short edge is nearest you). Roll out as big as the original rectangle. Fold the bottom third up and the top third down again. Press the edges. Wrap in plastic wrap and chill for 30 minutes. Repeat this rolling, folding, and turning four times, chilling well each time. Finally, chill the dough overnight.

Preheat the oven to 400°F/200°C. Grease two baking sheets. For the filling, mix the apples with the lemon rind and 3 tablespoons of the sugar. Roll out the dough into a 16-inch/40-cm square and cut into 16 squares. Pile a little of the apple filling in the center of each square, reserving any juice to glaze. Brush the edges with milk and fold the corners together into the center over the filling. Place on the baking sheets and chill for about 15 minutes.

Brush the pastries with the reserved juice and sprinkle with the remaining sugar. Bake for 10 minutes. Reduce the oven temperature to 350°F/180°C and bake for an additional 10–15 minutes, until browned.

makes 16

for the Danish pastry dough

2¹/2 cups white bread flour, plus extra for dusting

³/4 cup butter, well chilled, plus extra for greasing

¹/4 tsp salt

¹/4 oz/7 g active dry yeast

2 tbsp superfine sugar

1 egg, at room temperature

1 tsp vanilla extract

6 tbsp lukewarm water

beaten egg or milk, for glazing

for the filling

1 cup ground almonds

4 tbsp superfine sugar

1 egg, beaten

a few drops of almond extract

16 candied cherries

for the frosting

1 cup confectioners' sugar

a little water

cherry & almond windmills

For the Danish pastry dough, follow the instructions on page 11 as far as the final rolling, folding, and chilling stage.

Once the dough has chilled for several hours or overnight, prepare the filling. Mix together the almonds and sugar, then stir in the egg with a few drops of almond extract to make a paste. Divide the paste into 16 portions and roll them into balls.

Grease two baking sheets. Roll out the dough into a 16-inch/40-cm square and cut into 16 squares. For each square of dough, make a diagonal cut in from each corner, just over halfway toward the middle. Place a ball of almond paste in the center. Fold alternate corners to the middle, pressing them into the paste. Top with a cherry and place on a baking sheet. Chill for 15 minutes.

Meanwhile, preheat the oven to 400°F/200°C. Brush the windmills with a little beaten egg or milk and bake for 10 minutes. Reduce the temperature to 350°F/180°C and bake for an additional 5–10 minutes, until browned.

For the frosting, place the confectioners' sugar in a bowl and mix in a little water. Drizzle the frosting over the pastries as soon as they come out of the oven. Transfer to a wire rack and leave to cool completely.

makes 8

9 oz/250 g prepared puff pastry

milk, for glazing

for the filling

1 lb/450 g baking apples, peeled, cored, and chopped

grated rind of 1 lemon (optional)

pinch of ground cloves (optional)

3 tbsp sugar

for the orange sugar

1 tbsp sugar, for sprinkling

finely grated rind of 1 orange

for the orange cream

1 cup heavy cream

grated rind of 1 orange and juice of 1/2 orange

confectioners' sugar, to taste

apple turnovers

Prepare the filling before rolling out the pastry. Mix together the chopped apple, lemon rind, and ground cloves, if using, but do not add the sugar until the last minute because this will cause the juice to seep out of the apples. For the orange sugar, mix together the sugar and orange rind.

Preheat the oven to 425°F/220°C. Roll the pastry out on a floured surface into a rectangle measuring 24 x 12 inches/60 x 30 cm. Cut the pastry in half lengthwise, then across into four to make eight 6-inch/15-cm squares. (You can do this in two batches, rolling half of the pastry out into a 12-inch/30-cm square and cutting it into quarters, if preferred.)

Mix the sugar into the apple filling. Brush each square lightly with milk and place a little of the apple filling in the center. Fold one corner over diagonally to meet the opposite one, making a triangular turnover, and press the edges together very firmly. Place on a nonstick baking sheet. Repeat with the remaining squares.

Brush the turnovers with milk and sprinkle with a little of the orange sugar. Bake for 15–20 minutes, until puffed and well browned. Cool the turnovers on a wire rack.

For the orange cream, whip the cream and the orange rind and juice together until thick. Add a little sugar to taste and whip again until the cream just holds soft peaks. Serve the warm turnovers with dollops of orange cream.

makes 12

2 tbsp butter, cut into small pieces, plus extra for greasing

generous 1¹/₂ cups white bread flour

¹/₂ tsp salt

¹/₄ oz/7 g active dry yeast

1 egg, beaten lightly

¹/₂ cup tepid milk

2 tbsp maple syrup, for glazing

for the filling

4 tbsp butter, softened

2 tsp ground cinnamon

¹/₄ cup brown sugar

¹/₃ cup currants

cinnamon swirls

Grease a baking sheet with a little butter.

Sift the flour and salt into a mixing bowl. Stir in the yeast. Rub in the butter with your fingertips until the mixture resembles breadcrumbs. Add the egg and milk and mix to form a dough.

Form the dough into a ball, place in a greased bowl, cover, and let stand in a warm place for about 40 minutes or until doubled in size.

Punch down the dough lightly for 1 minute, then roll out to a rectangle measuring 12 x 9 inches/30 x 23 cm.

To make the filling, cream together the softened butter, cinnamon, and brown sugar until light and fluffy. Spread the filling evenly over the dough rectangle, leaving a 1-inch/2.5-cm border all around. Sprinkle the currants evenly over the top.

Roll up the dough from one of the long edges, and press down to seal. Cut the roll into 12 slices. Place them, cut-side down, on the baking sheet, cover, and let stand for 30 minutes.

Preheat the oven to 375°F/190°C. Bake the buns for 20–30 minutes, or until well risen. Brush with the maple syrup and let cool slightly before serving.

makes 24

4¹/₂ cups white bread flour,
plus extra for dusting

¹/₄ oz/7 g active dry yeast

¹/₂ cup superfine sugar

¹/₂ tsp salt

1 tsp ground cinnamon

6 tbsp butter

2 large eggs, plus 1 egg,
beaten, for glazing

1¹/₄ cups milk

oil, for greasing

for the filling

6 tbsp chocolate hazelnut
spread

7 oz/200 g milk chocolate,
chopped

double-chocolate swirls

Mix together the flour, yeast, sugar, salt, and cinnamon in a large bowl.

Melt the butter in a heatproof bowl set over a pan of gently simmering water, then allow to cool slightly. Whisk in the 2 eggs and milk. Pour into the flour mixture and mix well to form a dough.

Turn out onto a floured work counter and knead for 10 minutes until smooth. Put into a large floured bowl, cover with plastic wrap and put in a warm place for 8 hours, or overnight.

When you are ready to make the buns, take the dough from the bowl and punch down. Preheat the oven to 425°F/220°C and lightly oil 2 cookie sheets.

Divide the dough into 4 pieces and roll each piece into a rectangle about 1 inch/2.5 cm thick. Spread each rectangle with the chocolate hazelnut spread and scatter with the chopped chocolate. Roll up each piece from one of the long edges, then cut into 6 pieces. Place each swirl, cut-side down, on the cookie sheets and brush each one well with the beaten egg. Bake in the preheated oven for 20 minutes and serve warm.

serves 6

2 tbsp butter, cut into small pieces, plus extra for greasing

generous 1$\frac{1}{2}$ cups white bread flour

$\frac{1}{2}$ tsp salt

$\frac{1}{4}$ oz/7 g active dry yeast

$\frac{1}{2}$ cup tepid milk

1 egg, beaten lightly

for the filling

4 tbsp butter, softened

$\frac{1}{4}$ cup brown sugar

2 tbsp chopped hazelnuts

1 tbsp chopped preserved ginger

$\frac{1}{3}$ cup candied citrus peel

1 tbsp dark rum or cognac

for the frosting

1 cup confectioners' sugar

2 tbsp lemon juice

crown loaf

Grease a cookie sheet. Sift the flour and salt into a bowl. Stir in the yeast. Rub in the butter with your fingertips. Add the milk and egg and mix to form a dough.

Place the dough in a greased bowl, cover, and stand in a warm place for 40 minutes until doubled in size. Punch down the dough lightly for 1 minute. Roll out to a rectangle measuring about 12 x 9 inches/30 x 23 cm.

To make the filling, cream together the butter and sugar until light and fluffy. Stir in the hazelnuts, ginger, candied peel, and rum or cognac. Spread the filling over the dough, leaving a 1-inch/2.5-cm border.

Roll up the dough, starting from one of the long edges, into a sausage shape. Cut into slices at 2-inch/5-cm intervals and place, cut-side down, in a circle on the cookie sheet with the slices just touching. Cover and stand in a warm place to rise for 30 minutes.

Preheat the oven to 375°F/190°C. Bake the loaf for 20–30 minutes, or until golden. Meanwhile, mix the confectioners' sugar with enough lemon juice to form a thin frosting.

Let the loaf cool slightly before drizzling with frosting. Let the frosting set slightly before serving.

makes 12

3/4 cup butter, softened,
plus extra for greasing

4 cups white bread flour

1/2 tsp salt

1/4 oz/7 g active dry yeast

2 tbsp shortening

1 egg, beaten lightly

1 cup tepid water

31/2 oz/100 g semisweet
chocolate, broken into
12 squares

1 egg, beaten, for glazing

pain au chocolat

Lightly grease a cookie sheet. Sift the flour and salt into a mixing bowl and stir in the yeast. Rub in the shortening with your fingertips. Add the egg and enough of the water to mix to a soft dough. Knead for about 10 minutes to make a smooth elastic dough.

Roll out to a 15 x 8-inch/38 x 20-cm rectangle and mark it vertically into thirds. Divide the butter into 3 portions and dot one portion over the first two-thirds of the rectangle, leaving a small border around the edge.

Fold the rectangle into 3 by first folding the plain part of the dough over and then the other side. Seal the edges of the dough by pressing with a rolling pin. Give the dough a quarter-turn so the sealed edges are at the top and bottom. Roll out the dough as big as the original rectangle and fold (without adding butter), then wrap the dough and chill for 30 minutes.

Repeat this rolling, folding, and turning twice more until all of the butter has been used, chilling the dough each time. Re-roll and fold twice more without butter. Chill for a final 30 minutes.

Roll the dough out to 18 x 12 inches/45 x 30 cm, trim, and halve lengthwise. Cut each half into 6 rectangles and brush with beaten egg. Place a chocolate square at one end of each rectangle and roll up to form a sausage. Press the ends together and place, seam-side down, on the cookie sheet. Cover and let rise for 40 minutes in a warm place. Preheat the oven to 425°F/220°C. Brush each pastry roll with egg and bake in the preheated oven for 20–25 minutes, until golden. Cool on a wire rack. Serve warm or cold.

serves 6

for the puff pastry

1⅛ cups all-purpose flour

pinch of salt

¾ cup butter

about ⅔ cup chilled water

(or use 9 oz/250 g prepared
puff pastry)

for the filling

6–8 just-ripe peaches

scant ½ cup superfine sugar

3 heaping tbsp butter

3 pieces preserved ginger in
syrup, chopped

1 tbsp ginger syrup from the
preserved ginger jar

1 egg, beaten, for glazing

peach & ginger tarte tatin

To make the puff pastry, sift the flour and salt into a bowl and rub in 2 tbsp of the butter. Gradually add just enough water to bring the pastry together, and knead briefly to form a smooth dough. Wrap in plastic wrap and let chill for 30 minutes. Wrap the remaining butter in plastic wrap, and shape it into a 1¼-inch/ 3-cm thick rectangle. Roll out the dough to a rectangle 3 times longer and 1¼ inches/3 cm wider than the butter and place the butter in the center, long-side toward you. Fold over the 2 "wings" of dough to enclose the butter, press down the edges to seal, then turn the dough so the short side faces you. Roll the dough to its original length, fold into 3, turn, and roll again to its original length. Repeat this once more, then rewrap the dough and let chill again for 30 minutes. Remove from the refrigerator and repeat the rolling and turning twice more, then let chill again for 30 minutes.

Preheat the oven to 375°F/190°C. Plunge the peaches into boiling water, then let drain and peel. Cut each in half. Put the sugar in a 10-inch/25-cm heavy, ovenproof skillet and heat it gently until it caramelizes. Don't stir, just shake the skillet if necessary. Once the sugar turns a dark caramel color, remove from the heat, and drop 2 tbsp of the butter into it.

Place the peaches cut-side up on top of the caramel, packing them as close together as possible, and tucking the preserved ginger pieces into any gaps. Dot with the remaining butter and drizzle with the ginger syrup. Return to gentle heat while you roll out the dough in a circle larger than the skillet you are using. Drape the dough over the peaches and tuck it in well round the edges, brush with the beaten egg, and bake for 20–25 minutes, until the pastry is browned and puffed up. Remove from the oven and let rest for 5 minutes, then invert onto a plate and serve.

makes 6

for the puff pastry

1¹/₈ cups all-purpose flour

pinch of salt

³/₄ cup butter

about ²/₃ cup chilled water

(or use 9 oz/250 g prepared
puff pastry)

for the filling

1 large or 2 small eggplants,
trimmed and thinly sliced

5 tbsp olive oil

3 buffalo mozzarella balls,
sliced

6 tbsp pesto

black pepper

1 egg yolk, beaten, for glazing

6 slices prosciutto

eggplant, pesto & prosciutto tartlets

Prepare the puff pastry following the instructions on page 25.

When you are ready to make the tarts, cut the dough into 6, and roll into either circles or rectangles, then place on 2 baking sheets, 3 on each. Preheat the oven to 375°F/190°C.

Brush the eggplant slices with 2 tbsp of the olive oil and cook briefly in a nonstick skillet, in batches, then arrange the slices neatly overlapping on each dough base, leaving a 1-inch/2.5-cm margin round the edges. Lay the mozzarella slices over the eggplant slices and spoon over the pesto. Drizzle with the remaining olive oil and season with black pepper. Brush the edges of the dough with egg yolk and bake for 15 minutes. Remove from the oven and drape a slice of prosciutto on each tart before serving.

serves 6

for the puff pastry

1 cup all-purpose flour

pinch of salt

3/4 cup butter

about 2/3 cup chilled water

(or use 9 oz/250 g prepared
puff pastry)

for the topping

1 lb 2 oz/500 g goat cheese,
sliced

3–4 sprigs fresh thyme,
leaves picked from stalks

scant 1/3 cup black olives,
pitted

1 3/4 oz/50 g canned anchovies
in olive oil

1 tbsp olive oil

salt and pepper

1 egg yolk, beaten, for glazing

goat cheese & thyme tart

Prepare the puff pastry following the instructions on page 25.

Roll the dough into a large circle or rectangle and place on a baking sheet. Preheat the oven to 375°F/190°C.

Arrange the cheese slices on the dough, leaving a 1-inch/2.5-cm margin round the edge. Sprinkle the thyme and olives over the cheese and arrange the anchovies on top. Drizzle over the olive oil. Season well and brush the edges of the dough with the egg yolk. Bake for 20–25 minutes, until the cheese is bubbling and the pastry is browned.

So Choux

makes 12

for the choux pastry

5 tbsp butter, cut into small pieces, plus extra for greasing

2/3 cup water

3/4 cup all-purpose flour, sifted

2 eggs

for the pastry cream

2 eggs, beaten lightly

1/4 cup superfine sugar

2 tbsp cornstarch

1 1/4 cups milk

1/4 tsp vanilla extract

for the frosting

2 tbsp butter

1 tbsp milk

1 tbsp unsweetened cocoa

1/2 cup confectioners' sugar

1 3/4 oz/50 g white chocolate, broken into pieces

chocolate éclairs

Preheat the oven to 400°F/200°C. Lightly grease a cookie sheet. Place the water in a pan, add the butter, and heat gently until the butter melts. Bring to a rolling boil, then remove the pan from the heat and add the flour all at once, beating well until the mixture leaves the sides of the pan and forms a ball. Let cool slightly, then gradually beat in the eggs to form a smooth, glossy mixture. Spoon into a large pastry bag fitted with a 1/2-inch/1-cm plain tip.

Sprinkle the cookie sheet with a little water. Pipe éclairs 3 inches/ 7.5 cm long, spaced well apart. Bake in the preheated oven for 30–35 minutes, or until crisp and golden. Make a small slit in the side of each éclair to let the steam escape. Let cool on a wire rack.

Meanwhile, make the pastry cream. Whisk the eggs and sugar until thick and creamy, then fold in the cornstarch. Heat the milk until almost boiling and pour onto the eggs, whisking. Transfer to the pan and cook over low heat, stirring until thick. Remove the pan from the heat and stir in the vanilla extract. Cover with parchment paper and let cool.

To make the frosting, melt the butter with the milk in a pan, remove from the heat and stir in the unsweetened cocoa and sugar. Split the éclairs lengthwise and pipe in the pastry cream. Spread the frosting over the top of the éclair. Melt a little white chocolate in a heatproof bowl set over a pan of gently simmering water, then spoon over the chocolate frosting, swirl in, and let set.

makes 12

for the choux pastry

4 tbsp butter

2/3 cup water

1/2 cup all-purpose flour, sifted

2 eggs, beaten

for the filling and topping

3/4 cup heavy cream

1 tbsp confectioners' sugar

3/4 cup fresh raspberries

3 oz/85 g semisweet chocolate, broken into pieces

raspberry chocolate éclairs

Preheat the oven to 425°F/220°C. To make the dough, place the butter and water in a heavy-bottom pan and bring to a boil over low heat. Add the flour, all at once, and beat thoroughly until the mixture leaves the side of the pan. Let cool slightly, then vigorously beat in the eggs, a little at a time.

Spoon the mixture into a pastry bag fitted with a ½-inch/1-cm tip and pipe 3-inch/7.5-cm lengths onto a dampened cookie sheet. Bake in the preheated oven for 10 minutes, then reduce the oven temperature to 375°F/190°C and bake for an additional 20 minutes, or until crisp and golden brown. Split the side of each éclair to let the steam escape, and transfer to a wire rack to cool completely.

To make the filling, place the cream and confectioners' sugar in a bowl and whip until thick. Split the éclairs lengthwise and spoon in the cream mixture. Place a few raspberries in each éclair.

Melt the chocolate in a heatproof bowl set over a pan of gently simmering water. Spread a little on top of each éclair. Let set, then serve.

makes 12

for the choux pastry

²/₃ cup water

4 tbsp butter, plus extra
for greasing

³/₄ cup all-purpose flour,
sifted

2 eggs, lightly beaten

for the filling

1¹/₄ cups heavy cream

4 tbsp rum

1 tbsp confectioners' sugar

for the coffee caramel

1 cup sugar

¹/₂ cup water

1 tsp instant coffee

coffee caramel éclairs

Place the water and butter in a pan and heat gently until the butter melts, then turn up the heat and bring it rapidly to a boil. Immediately add all the flour, remove the pan from the heat, and stir the mixture into a paste that leaves the sides of the pan clean. Do not beat or it will become greasy. Allow to cool slightly for about 15 minutes.

Meanwhile, preheat the oven to 425°F/220°C. Grease a baking sheet and prepare a piping bag fitted with a plain ³/₄-inch/1.5-cm tube. Gradually beat the eggs into the flour paste and continue beating until it is smooth and glossy. Spoon the paste into the bag and pipe 12 strips of paste on the baking sheet.

Bake for 15 minutes. Reduce the oven temperature to 375°F/ 190°C and cook for an additional 20–25 minutes, until the éclairs are risen, well browned, and crisp. Transfer to a wire rack, slitting each pastry lengthwise to allow the steam to escape. Leave to cool.

For the filling, whip the cream with the rum and confectioners' sugar. Pipe this into the pastries and return them to the wire rack placing it over a baking sheet. Keep the pastries close together.

For the caramel, place the sugar in a pan and add the water. Heat gently, stirring occasionally, until the sugar has dissolved. Then bring to a boil and boil rapidly, without stirring, until the syrup turns golden. Remove from the heat and stir in the coffee using a metal fork. Immediately drizzle the coffee caramel over the éclairs. Leave to set and cool, then use kitchen scissors to snip any drizzles of set caramel between the éclairs.

white chocolate passion éclairs

makes 12

for the choux pastry

2/3 cup water

4 tbsp butter, plus extra for greasing

3/4 cup all-purpose flour, sifted

2 eggs, lightly beaten

for the filling and topping

4 passion fruit

1 1/2 cups mascarpone cheese

14 oz/400 g white chocolate

crystallized rose petals or violets, to decorate (optional)

Place the water and butter in a pan and heat gently until the butter melts, then turn up the heat and bring it rapidly to a boil. Immediately add all the flour, remove the pan from the heat, and stir the mixture into a paste that leaves the sides of the pan clean. Do not beat or it will become greasy. Allow to cool slightly for about 15 minutes.

Meanwhile, preheat the oven to 425°F/220°C. Grease a baking sheet and prepare a piping bag fitted with a plain 3/4-inch/1.5-cm tube. Gradually beat the eggs into the flour paste and continue beating until it is smooth and glossy. Spoon the paste into the bag and pipe 12 strips of paste on the baking sheet.

Bake for 15 minutes. Reduce the oven temperature to 375°F/190°C and cook for an additional 20–25 minutes, until the éclairs are risen, well browned and crisp. Transfer to a wire rack, slitting each pastry lengthwise to allow the steam to escape. Leave to cool.

Halve the passion fruit and scoop out the flesh into a strainer over a bowl. Press out all the juice and discard the seeds. Mix the juice into the mascarpone.

Melt 6 oz/175 g of the chocolate in a heatproof bowl over a pan of gently simmering water, stirring occasionally. Stir this into the mascarpone. Melt the remaining chocolate.

Fill the éclairs with the mascarpone mixture. Coat the tops with the melted white chocolate. Add a little piece of crystallized rose petal or violet on top of each, if using, and leave to set before serving.

strawberry petits choux

makes 12

for the filling and topping

2 tsp powdered gelatin

2 tbsp water

3 cups strawberries, hulled

1 cup ricotta cheese

1 tbsp superfine sugar

2 tsp strawberry-flavored liqueur

confectioners' sugar, for dusting

for the petits choux

3/4 cup all-purpose flour

2 tbsp unsweetened cocoa

pinch of salt

6 tbsp butter

1 cup water

2 eggs, plus 1 egg white, beaten

Sprinkle the gelatin over the water in a heatproof bowl. Let it soften for 2–3 minutes. Place the bowl over a pan of gently simmering water and stir until the gelatin dissolves. Remove from the heat.

Place a scant 1 cup of the strawberries in a blender with the ricotta, sugar, and liqueur. Process until blended. Add the gelatin and process briefly. Transfer the mousse to a bowl, cover with plastic wrap, and chill for 1–1½ hours, until set.

Meanwhile, make the petits choux. Line a cookie sheet with parchment paper. Sift together the flour, unsweetened cocoa, and salt. Put the butter and water into a heavy-bottom pan and heat gently until the butter has melted.

Preheat the oven to 425°F/220°C. Remove the pan from the heat and add the flour, unsweetened cocoa, and salt all at once, stirring well until the mixture leaves the sides of the pan. Leave to cool slightly.

Gradually beat the eggs into the flour paste and continue beating until it is smooth and glossy. Drop 12 rounded tablespoonfuls of the mixture onto the prepared cookie sheet and bake for 20–25 minutes, until puffed up and crisp.

Remove from the oven and make a slit in the side of each petit chou. Return to the oven for 5 minutes. Transfer to a wire rack.

Slice the remaining strawberries. Cut the petits choux in half, divide the mousse and strawberry slices among them, then replace the tops. Dust lightly with confectioners' sugar and place in the refrigerator. Serve within 1½ hours.

serves 4

for the choux pastry

5 tbsp butter, plus extra for greasing

generous ¾ cup water

¾ cup all-purpose flour

3 eggs, beaten

for the cream filling

1¼ cups heavy cream

3 tbsp superfine sugar

1 tsp vanilla extract

for the chocolate sauce

4½ oz/125 g semisweet chocolate, broken into small pieces

2½ tbsp butter

6 tbsp water

2 tbsp brandy

profiteroles with chocolate sauce

Preheat the oven to 400°F/200°C. Grease a large cookie sheet with butter. To make the pastry, put the water and butter into a pan and bring to a boil. Meanwhile, sift the flour into a bowl. Immediately add all the flour, remove the pan from the heat, and stir the mixture into a paste that leaves the sides of the saucepan clean. Leave to cool slightly. Beat in enough of the eggs to give the mixture a soft, dropping consistency.

Transfer into a pastry bag fitted with a ½-inch/1-cm plain tip. Pipe small balls onto the cookie sheet. Bake for 25 minutes. Remove from the oven. Pierce each ball with a skewer to let the steam escape.

To make the filling, whip together the cream, sugar, and vanilla extract. Cut the pastry balls almost in half, then fill with cream.

To make the sauce, gently melt the chocolate and butter with the water in a heatproof bowl set over a saucepan of gently simmering water, stirring, until smooth. Stir in the brandy. Pile the profiteroles into individual serving dishes or into a pyramid on a raised cake stand. Pour over the sauce and serve.

makes 4

for the choux pastry

2/3 cup water

4 tbsp butter, plus extra for greasing

3/4 cup all-purpose flour, sifted

2 eggs, lightly beaten

1/4 cup slivered almonds

for the filling

grated rind of 2 lemons

2 tbsp confectioners' sugar, plus extra for dusting

1 1/2 cups lowfat sour cream

juice of 1/2 lemon

blueberries, raspberries, or strawberries, to serve (optional)

lemon cheesecake rings

Place the water and butter in a pan and heat gently until the butter melts, then turn up the heat and bring it rapidly to a boil. Immediately add all the flour, remove the pan from the heat, and stir the mixture into a paste that leaves the sides of the pan clean. Do not beat or it will become greasy. Set aside for about 15 minutes to cool slightly.

Preheat the oven to 425°F/220°C. Grease a baking sheet. Gradually beat the egg into the flour paste and continue beating until the mixture is smooth and glossy. Spoon dollops of the paste onto the baking sheet, shaping it into 4 rings of about 4 inches/10 cm in diameter, making sure that they are well spaced. Sprinkle with slivered almonds and press them gently onto the paste with the point of a knife.

Bake for 15 minutes. Reduce the oven temperature to 350°F/180°C and cook for an additional 20–25 minutes, until the rings are risen, well browned, and crisp. Transfer to a wire rack, and use a serrated knife to slice each ring horizontally in half. Leave to cool.

For the filling, place the lemon rind, confectioners' sugar, and sour cream in a bowl and mix well, adding lemon juice to taste. Let chill until ready to serve the rings. Spoon or pipe the filling on the bottom layers of the rings and replace the tops. Sift over a little confectioner's sugar and serve with the soft fruit, if using.

makes 20

for the choux fritters

1 lb 4 oz/540 g can pineapple
pieces in natural juice

4 tbsp butter

3/4 cup all-purpose flour,
sifted

2 eggs, lightly beaten

grated rind of 1 orange

oil, for deep-frying

for the ginger-wine honey

1 tsp arrowroot or cornstarch

4 tbsp ginger wine

3 tbsp clear honey

2 pieces preserved ginger,
cut into slivers

pineapple choux fritters

Drain the pineapple, reserving the juice. Check through the pineapple pieces, snipping any large ones in half with kitchen scissors, and set aside. Measure ⅔ cup of the pineapple juice into a pan. Add the butter and heat gently until the butter melts, then turn up the heat and bring rapidly to a boil. Immediately add all the flour, remove the pan from the heat, and stir the mixture into a paste that leaves the sides of the pan clean. Do not beat or it will become greasy. Allow to cool slightly for about 15 minutes.

Meanwhile, for the ginger-wine honey, mix the arrowroot or cornstarch to a paste with the ginger wine in a small pan, then stir in the honey. Bring to a boil, stirring continuously, and remove from the heat. Stir in the preserved ginger. Set aside.

Heat the oil for deep-frying to 375°F/190°C or until a cube of bread browns in about 1 minute. Beat the eggs into the flour paste, then beat in the orange rind until the paste is glossy. Stir in the pineapple until just mixed.

Deep-fry spoonfuls of the pineapple mixture turning once or twice, for 3–5 minutes, until puffed and golden. Drain on paper towels and keep warm until all the fritters are cooked. Pile the choux fritters into dishes. Stir the ginger-wine honey and drizzle it over the fritters. Serve at once.

makes 22

for the choux pastry

4 tbsp butter, plus extra
for greasing

2/3 cup water

1/2 cup all-purpose flour,
sifted

2 eggs, beaten

for the filling

2 tbsp mayonnaise

1 tsp tomato paste

5 oz/140 g small shrimp,
cooked and peeled

1 tsp Worcestershire sauce

salt

Tabasco sauce

1 head Boston lettuce,
shredded

cayenne pepper, to garnish

mini choux puffs with shrimp cocktail

Preheat the oven to 350°F/180°C, then grease a cookie sheet. To make the choux pastry, place the butter and water in a large, heavy-bottom pan and bring to a boil. Immediately add all the flour, remove the pan from the heat, and stir the mixture into a paste that leaves the sides of the pan clean. Let cool slightly, then vigorously beat in the eggs, one at a time. Place 22 walnut-size spoonfuls of the mixture onto the cookie sheet, spaced 3/4 inch/2 cm apart. Bake in the preheated oven for 35 minutes, or until light, crisp, and golden. Transfer to a wire rack to cool, then cut a 1/4-inch/5-mm slice from the top of each puff.

To make the filling, place the mayonnaise, tomato paste, shrimp, and Worcestershire sauce in a bowl. Add salt and Tabasco sauce to taste, and mix together until combined.

Place a few lettuce shreds in the bottom of each puff, making sure some protrude at the top. Spoon the shrimp mixture on top and dust with a little cayenne pepper before serving.

makes 24

²/₃ cup water

4 tbsp butter, plus extra
for greasing

³/₄ cup all-purpose flour,
sifted

2 eggs, lightly beaten

4 tbsp finely chopped
scallions

grated rind of 1 lemon

1 garlic clove, crushed

1³/₄ oz/50 g bleu cheese,
finely crumbled

24 pitted black olives

bleu cheese & olive gougères

Place the water and butter in a saucepan and heat gently until the butter melts, then turn up the heat and bring it rapidly to a boil. Immediately add all the flour, remove the pan from the heat, and stir the mixture into a paste that leaves the sides of the pan clean. Do not beat or it will become greasy. Allow to cool slightly for about 15 minutes.

Meanwhile, preheat the oven to 425°F/220°C. Grease two baking sheets. Gradually beat the eggs into the flour paste, then beat in the scallions, lemon rind, and garlic until the paste is smooth and glossy. Beat in the bleu cheese.

Use two teaspoons to spoon small mounds of the mixture on the baking sheets (or pipe it from a bag with a plain nozzle). Press an olive into each mound. Bake for about 20 minutes, until well risen, crisp, and browned. Transfer to a wire rack and cool briefly before serving hot, warm, or cold.

3

Fancy Filo

makes 4

1 apple

1 ripe pear

2 tbsp lemon juice

4 tbsp butter

4 sheets filo pastry, thawed if frozen

2 tbsp apricot jelly

1 tbsp orange juice

1 tbsp chopped pistachio

2 tsp confectioners' sugar, for dusting

paper-thin fruit pies

Preheat the oven to 400°F/200°C. Core and thinly slice the apple and pear and immediately toss them in the lemon juice to prevent them from turning brown. Melt the butter in a pan over low heat.

Cut each sheet of pastry into 4 and cover with a clean, damp dish towel. Brush a 4-cup nonstick muffin pan (cup size 4 inches/10 cm in diameter) with a little of the butter.

Working on each pie separately, brush 4 small sheets of pastry with butter. Press a sheet of pastry into the base of 1 cup. Arrange the other sheets of pastry on top at slightly different angles. Repeat with the other sheets of pastry to make another 3 pies.

Arrange the apple and pear slices alternately in the center of each pie shell and lightly crimp the edge of the pastry of each pie.

Stir the jelly and orange juice together until smooth and brush over the fruit. Bake in the preheated oven for 12–15 minutes. Sprinkle with the pistachios, dust lightly with confectioners' sugar, and serve hot straight from the oven.

makes 25

2 cups walnut halves

1³/4 cups shelled pistachios

³/4 cup blanched almonds

4 tbsp pine nuts, chopped finely

finely grated rind of 2 large oranges

6 tbsp sesame seeds

1 tbsp sugar

¹/2 tsp ground cinnamon

¹/2 tsp allspice

1 cup butter, melted, plus extra for greasing

23 sheets filo pastry, thawed if frozen

for the syrup

3 cups superfine sugar

2 cups water

5 tbsp honey

3 cloves

2 large strips lemon rind

baklava

To make the filling, put the walnuts, pistachios, almonds, and pine nuts in a food processor and process gently, until finely chopped but not ground. Transfer the chopped nuts to a bowl and stir in the orange rind, sesame seeds, sugar, cinnamon, and allspice.

Grease a 10-inch/25-cm square (or similar) ovenproof dish that is 2 inches/5 cm deep. Preheat the oven to 325°F/160°C. Cut the stacked filo sheets to size, using a ruler. Keep the sheets covered with a damp dish towel. Place a sheet of filo on the bottom of the dish and brush with melted butter. Top with 7 more sheets, brushing with butter between each layer.

Sprinkle with 1 cup of the filling. Top with 3 sheets of filo, brushing each one with butter. Continue layering until you have used up all the filo and filling, ending with a top layer of 3 sheets of filo. Brush with butter.

Using a sharp knife and a ruler, cut the baklava into 2-inch/5-cm squares. Brush again with butter. Bake in the preheated oven for 1 hour.

Meanwhile, put all the syrup ingredients in a pan, stirring to dissolve the sugar. Bring to a boil, then simmer for 15 minutes, without stirring, until a thin syrup forms. Cool.

Remove the baklava from the oven and pour the syrup over the top. Let set in the dish, then remove the squares to serve.

makes 18

2 oz/55 g semisweet
chocolate, broken into pieces

3/4 cup ground hazelnuts

1 tbsp finely chopped
fresh mint

1/2 cup sour cream

2 apples

9 sheets filo pastry, about
6 inches/15 cm square,
thawed if frozen

4–6 tbsp butter, melted

confectioners' sugar,
for dusting

chocolate filo parcels

Preheat the oven to 375°F/190°C. Break up the chocolate and melt in a heatproof bowl set over a pan of gently simmering water. Remove from the heat and let cool slightly.

Mix together the hazelnuts, mint, and sour cream in a bowl. Peel the apples and grate them into the bowl, then stir in the melted chocolate and mix well.

Cut each sheet of filo pastry into 4 squares. Keep the squares you are not using covered with a damp dish towel. Brush 1 square with melted butter, place a second square on top, and brush with melted butter. Place a tablespoonful of the chocolate mixture in the center, then bring up the corners of the squares and twist together to enclose the filling completely. Continue making parcels in the same way until you have used up all the pastry and filling.

Brush a cookie sheet with melted butter and place the parcels on it. Bake for about 10 minutes, until crisp and golden. Let cool slightly, then dust with confectioners' sugar.

makes 20

4 tbsp butter, melted,
plus extra for greasing

10 sheets filo pastry,
thawed if frozen

for the filling

1/2 cup pistachios,
ground coarsely

1/2 cup ground hazelnuts

2 tbsp granulated sugar

1 tbsp rose water

2 oz/55 g semisweet
chocolate, grated

confectioners' sugar,
for dusting

pistachio pastries

Preheat the oven to 350°F/180°C. Grease 2 cookie sheets. To make the filling, put the pistachios and hazelnuts in a bowl with the sugar, rose water, and chocolate. Mix together. Cut each sheet of filo pastry lengthwise in half. Pile the rectangles on top of each other and cover with a dish towel to prevent them from drying out.

Brush a filo sheet with melted butter. Spread a teaspoon of filling along one short end. Fold the long sides in, slightly over the filling and roll up from the filling end. Place on the prepared cookie sheets with the seam underneath and brush with melted butter.

Repeat with the remaining pastry and filling. Bake in the preheated oven for 20 minutes, or until crisp and very lightly colored. Transfer to a wire rack to cool. Dust with confectioners' sugar before serving.

serves 2–4

8 crisp apples

1 tbsp lemon juice

2/3 cup golden raisins

1 tsp ground cinnamon

1/2 tsp grated nutmeg

1 tbsp brown sugar

6 sheets filo pastry, thawed if frozen

vegetable oil spray

confectioners' sugar, to serve

for the sauce

1 tbsp cornstarch

2 cups hard cider

apple strudel & cider sauce

Preheat the oven to 375°F/190°C. Line a baking sheet with parchment paper.

Peel and core the apples and chop them into ½-inch/1-cm dice. Toss the apples in a bowl with the lemon juice, golden raisins, cinnamon, nutmeg, and brown sugar.

Lay out a sheet of filo pastry, spray with vegetable oil, and lay a second sheet on top. Repeat with a third sheet. Spread over half the apple mixture and roll up lengthwise, tucking in the ends to enclose the filling. Repeat to make a second strudel. Slide onto the baking sheet, spray with oil, and bake for 15–20 minutes.

To make the sauce, blend the cornstarch in a pan with a little hard cider until smooth. Add the remaining cider and heat gently, stirring, until the mixture boils and thickens. Serve the strudel warm or cold, dredged with confectioners' sugar, and accompanied by the cider sauce.

serves 4

2 ripe pears

4 tbsp butter

1 cup fresh white breadcrumbs

1/3 cup shelled pecans, chopped

1/8 cup light brown sugar

finely grated rind of 1 orange

31/2 oz/100 g filo pastry, thawed if frozen

6 tbsp orange blossom honey

2 tbsp orange juice

confectioners' sugar, for dusting

strained plain yogurt, to serve (optional)

pear & pecan strudel

Preheat the oven to 400°F/200°C. Peel, core, and chop the pears. Melt 1 tablespoon of the butter in a skillet and gently sauté the breadcrumbs until golden. Transfer the breadcrumbs to a bowl and add the pears, nuts, sugar, and orange rind. Place the remaining butter in a small pan and heat until melted.

Set aside 1 sheet of filo pastry, keeping it well wrapped, and brush the remaining filo sheets with a little melted butter. Spoon a little of the nut filling onto the first filo sheet, leaving a 1-inch/2.5-cm margin around the edge. Build up the strudel by placing buttered filo sheets on top of the first, spreading each one with nut filling as you build up the layers. Drizzle the honey and orange juice over the top.

Fold the short ends over the filling, then roll up, starting at a long side. Carefully lift onto a baking sheet, with the seam on top. Brush with any remaining melted butter and crumple the reserved sheet of filo pastry around the strudel. Bake for 25 minutes, or until golden and crisp. Dust with confectioners' sugar and serve warm with strained plain yogurt, if using.

serves 6

³/₄ cup butter, plus extra
for greasing

generous 1¹/₄ cups mixed
chopped nuts

4 oz/115 g semisweet
chocolate, chopped

4 oz/115 g milk chocolate,
chopped

4 oz/115 g white chocolate,
chopped

7 oz/200 g filo pastry, thawed
if frozen

3 tbsp corn syrup

¹/₂ cup confectioners' sugar

chocolate nut strudel

Preheat the oven to 375°F/190°C. Lightly grease a baking sheet with butter. Set aside 1 tablespoon of the nuts. Place the remaining nuts in a bowl and mix together with the 3 types of chocolate.

Place 1 sheet of filo pastry on a clean dish towel. Melt the butter and brush the sheet of filo with the butter, drizzle with a little syrup, and sprinkle with some nuts and chocolate. Place another sheet of filo on top and repeat until you have used all the nuts and chocolate.

Use the dish towel to help you carefully roll up the strudel and place on the baking sheet, drizzle with a little more syrup, and sprinkle with the reserved nuts. Bake in the preheated oven for 20–25 minutes. If the nuts start to brown too much, cover the strudel with a sheet of foil. Sprinkle the strudel with confectioners' sugar, slice, and serve.

makes 12

1 banana

1 oz/25 g chocolate chips

4 sheets filo pastry, thawed if frozen

4 tbsp butter, melted

for the chocolate sauce

2/3 cup light cream

2 oz/55 g semisweet chocolate, broken into pieces

banana & chocolate triangles

Preheat the oven to 350°F/180°C. Peel the banana, put in a bowl and mash with a fork. Stir in the chocolate chips. Cover the filo sheets with a dish towel to prevent them from drying out. Brush a filo sheet with melted butter and cut lengthwise into 3 strips, each about 2½ inches/6 cm wide.

Spoon a little of the banana mixture onto the bottom end of each strip, fold the corner of the pastry over to enclose it in a triangle, and continue folding along the whole length of the strip to make a triangular parcel. Place on a cookie sheet with the seam underneath. Repeat with the remaining pastry and filling. Bake in the preheated oven for 10–12 minutes, until golden.

To make the chocolate sauce, put the cream and chocolate in a heatproof bowl set over a pan of gently simmering water and stir until the chocolate has melted. Serve the pastries with the chocolate sauce.

makes 20

for the tartlet shells

2$^1/_2$ oz/70 g filo pastry,
thawed if frozen

3 tbsp melted butter, plus
extra for greasing

for the avocado salsa

1 large avocado

1 small red onion,
finely chopped

1 fresh chile, seeded and
finely chopped

2 tomatoes, peeled, seeded,
and finely chopped

juice of 1 lime

2 tbsp chopped fresh cilantro

salt and pepper

filo tartlets with avocado salsa

Preheat the oven to 350°F/180°C. To make the tartlet shells, working with 1 sheet of filo pastry at a time and keeping the rest covered with a damp cloth, brush the pastry sheet with melted butter. With a sharp knife, cut the sheet into 2-inch/5-cm squares.

Grease 20 cups in mini muffin pans and line each one with 3 buttered filo pastry squares, setting each one at an angle to the others. Repeat until all the pastry is used up. Bake in the preheated oven for 6–8 minutes, or until crisp and golden. Carefully transfer to a wire rack to cool.

To make the salsa, peel the avocado and remove the pit. Cut the flesh into small cubes and place in a bowl with the onion, chile, tomatoes, lime juice, and cilantro, and add salt and pepper to taste. Divide the avocado salsa among the tartlet shells and serve immediately.

makes 12

6 tbsp butter, melted,
plus extra for greasing

7 oz/200 g fresh or canned
crabmeat, drained

6 scallions, finely chopped

1-inch/2.5-cm piece of fresh
ginger, peeled and grated

2 tsp soy sauce

pepper

12 sheets filo pastry,
thawed if frozen

crab & ginger triangles

Preheat the oven to 350°F/180°C, then grease a cookie sheet. Place the crabmeat, scallions, ginger, and soy sauce in a bowl, add pepper to taste, mix together, and reserve. Working with 1 sheet of filo pastry at a time and keeping the rest covered with a damp cloth, brush a pastry sheet with melted butter, fold in half lengthwise and brush again with butter.

Place a spoonful of the crab mixture in one corner of the pastry strip. Fold the pastry and filling over at right angles to make a triangle enclosing the filling. Continue folding in this way all the way down the strip to make a triangular pocket.

Place the pocket on the prepared cookie sheet. Repeat with the remaining pastry and crab mixture. Brush each parcel with melted butter. Bake in the preheated oven for 20–25 minutes, or until crisp and golden brown. Serve warm.

Short & Simple

makes 6

for the pie dough

scant 1¼ cups all-purpose flour

pinch of salt

4 tbsp butter, cut into small pieces

4 tbsp lard or vegetable shortening, cut into small pieces

2–3 tbsp cold water

for the filling

4 tbsp cornstarch

1¾ cups canned coconut milk

grated rind and juice of 2 limes

2 eggs, separated

scant 1 cup superfine sugar

lime & coconut meringue pies

To make the pie dough, sift the flour and salt into a large bowl and rub in the butter and fat with your fingertips until the mixture resembles breadcrumbs. Add a little water and work the mixture together until a soft dough has formed. Wrap the dough and let chill in the refrigerator for 30 minutes.

Preheat the oven to 350°F/180°C. Roll out the pie dough and use to line 6 tart pans, each 4 inches/10 cm in diameter and 1½ inches/3 cm deep. Line with parchment paper and dried beans. Bake in the oven for 15 minutes. Remove from the oven and take out the paper and beans. Reduce the oven temperature to 325°F/160°C.

To make the filling, place the cornstarch in a pan with a little of the coconut milk and stir to make a smooth paste. Stir in the rest of the coconut milk. Gradually bring to a boil over low heat, stirring constantly. Cook, stirring, for 3 minutes until thickened. Remove from the heat and add the lime rind and juice, egg yolks, and 4 tablespoons of the sugar. Pour the mixture into the pastry shells.

Place the egg whites in a clean, greasefree bowl and whisk until very stiff, then gradually whisk in the remaining sugar, keeping a firm consistency. Pipe the meringue into peaks over the filling to cover it completely or cover the filling with the meringue and swirl gently with a spatula. Bake the pies in the oven for 20 minutes, or until the tops are lightly browned. Serve hot or cold.

makes 12

for the dough

scant 1¹/₂ cups all-purpose flour, plus extra for dusting

³/₄ cup confectioners' sugar

²/₃ cup ground almonds

¹/₂ cup butter

1 egg yolk

1 tbsp milk

for the filling

1 cup cream cheese

confectioners' sugar, to taste, plus extra for dusting

12 oz/350 g fresh summer fruits, such as blueberries, raspberries, and small strawberries

summer fruit tartlets

To make the dough, sift the flour and confectioners' sugar into a bowl. Stir in the ground almonds. Add the butter and rub in until the mixture resembles breadcrumbs. Add the egg yolk and milk and work in with a spatula, then mix with your fingers until the dough binds together. Wrap the dough in plastic wrap and let chill in the refrigerator for 30 minutes.

Preheat the oven to 400°F/200°C. On a floured counter, roll out the dough and use to line 12 deep tartlet or individual brioche pans. Prick the bottoms. Press a piece of foil into each tartlet, covering the edges, and bake in the preheated oven for 10–15 minutes, or until light golden brown. Remove the foil and bake for an additional 2–3 minutes. Transfer to a wire rack to cool.

To make the filling, place the cream cheese and confectioners' sugar in a bowl and mix together. Place a spoonful of filling in each tart shell and arrange the fruit on top. Dust with sifted confectioners' sugar and serve.

makes 12

for the pie dough

1 cup all-purpose flour, plus extra for dusting

6 tbsp butter, cut into small pieces

1/4 cup superfine sugar

2 egg yolks

for the filling

2 tbsp maple syrup

2/3 cup heavy cream

1/2 cup superfine sugar

pinch of cream of tartar

6 tbsp water

1 cup shelled pecans, chopped

12–24 pecan halves, to decorate

maple pecan pies

To make the pie dough, sift the flour into a mixing bowl and rub in the butter with your fingertips until the mixture resembles breadcrumbs. Add the sugar and egg yolks and mix to form a soft dough. Wrap the dough and let chill in the refrigerator for 30 minutes. Preheat the oven to 400°F/200°C.

On a lightly floured counter, roll out the pie dough thinly, cut out 12 circles, and use to line 12 tartlet pans. Prick the bases with a fork. Line with parchment paper and fill with dried beans. Bake in the oven for 10–15 minutes, or until light golden. Remove from the oven and take out the paper and beans. Bake the pastry shells for an additional 2–3 minutes. Let cool on a wire rack.

Mix half the maple syrup and half the cream in a bowl. Place the sugar, cream of tartar, and water in a pan and heat gently until the sugar dissolves. Bring to a boil and boil until light golden. Remove from the heat and stir in the maple syrup and cream mixture.

Return the pan to the heat and cook to the soft ball stage (240°F/116°C): that is, when a little of the mixture dropped into a bowl of cold water forms a soft ball. Stir in the remaining cream and leave until cool. Brush the remaining maple syrup over the edges of the pies. Place the chopped pecans in the pastry shells and spoon in the toffee. Top each pie with 1 or 2 pecan halves. Let cool completely before serving.

florentine praline tartlets

makes 6

for the praline

1/2 cup sugar

3 tbsp water

scant 1/2 cup slivered almonds

butter, for greasing

for the pie dough

3/4 cup all-purpose flour, plus extra for dusting

pinch of salt

5 tbsp butter, cut into pieces

1 tsp confectioners' sugar

cold water

for the frangipane

5 tbsp butter

2 eggs

1/3 cup superfine sugar

2 tbsp all-purpose flour

1 cup ground almonds

for the topping

8 candied cherries, chopped, plus extra to decorate

2 tbsp mixed candied citrus peel, chopped

31/2 oz/100 g semisweet chocolate, chopped

First make the praline. Put the sugar and the water in a pan and dissolve the sugar over low heat. Do not stir the sugar, just let it boil for 10 minutes, until it turns to caramel, then stir in the slivered almonds and turn out onto buttered foil. Let cool and harden. When cold, break up the praline and chop into smallish pieces.

Grease six 3½-inch/9-cm loose-bottom fluted tart pans. Sift the flour and salt into a food processor, add the butter, and process until the mixture resembles fine breadcrumbs. Tip the mixture into a large bowl, add the confectioners' sugar and a little cold water, just enough to bring the dough together. Turn out onto a floured counter and divide into 6 equal-size pieces. Roll each piece to fit the tart pans. Carefully fit each piece of dough in its shell and press well to fit the pan. Roll the rolling pin over the pan to neaten the edges and trim the excess dough. Put in the freezer for 30 minutes. Meanwhile, preheat the oven to 400°F/200°C.

While the tarts are in the freezer, make the frangipane. Melt the butter and beat the eggs and superfine sugar together. Stir the melted butter into the egg and sugar mixture, then add the flour and ground almonds. Remove the tart tins from the freezer. Line with baking paper and dried beans and bake for 10 minutes. Remove the paper and beans, then divide the frangipane among the tart shells and return to the oven for 8–10 minutes.

While the tarts are baking, mix the cherries, peel, chocolate, and praline together. Divide among the tarts while they are still hot so that some of the chocolate melts. Serve cold, decorated with candied cherries.

makes 12

for the pie dough

generous 1 cup all-purpose
flour, plus extra for dusting

2 tbsp superfine sugar

3/4 cup butter, diced

2 egg yolks

2 tbsp cold water

for the filling and topping

1 vanilla bean

1 3/4 cups heavy cream

12 oz/350 g white chocolate,
broken into pieces

semisweet chocolate curls,
to decorate

unsweetened cocoa,
for dusting

white chocolate tarts

Place the flour and sugar in a bowl. Add the butter and rub it in until the mixture resembles fine breadcrumbs. Place the egg yolks and water in a separate bowl and mix together. Stir into the dry ingredients and mix to form a dough. Knead for 1 minute, or until smooth. Wrap in plastic wrap and let chill for 20 minutes.

Preheat the oven to 400°F/200°C. Roll out the dough on a floured work counter and use to line 12 tartlet molds. Prick the bases, cover, and let chill for 15 minutes. Line the cases with foil and dried beans and bake for 10 minutes. Remove the beans and foil and cook for an additional 5 minutes. Let cool.

To make the filling, split the vanilla bean lengthwise and scrape out the black seeds with a knife. Place the seeds in a pan with the cream and heat until almost boiling. Melt the chocolate in a heatproof bowl set over a pan of gently simmering water, then pour over the hot cream. Keep stirring until smooth. Whisk the mixture with an electric mixer until thickened and the beater leaves a trail when lifted. Let chill in the refrigerator for 30 minutes, then whip until soft peaks form. Divide the filling among the pastry shells and let chill for 30 minutes. Decorate with chocolate curls and dust with unsweetened cocoa.

makes 10

for the pie dough

scant 1¹/4 cups all-purpose
flour

¹/2 cup unsweetened cocoa

¹/4 cup superfine sugar

pinch of salt

¹/2 cup butter, cut into
small pieces

1 egg yolk

1–2 tbsp cold water

for the sauce

1¹/2 cups blueberries

2 tbsp crème de cassis

scant ¹/8 cup confectioners'
sugar, sifted

for the filling

5 oz/140 g semisweet
chocolate

1 cup heavy cream

²/3 cup sour cream

chocolate blueberry pies

To make the pie dough, place the flour, cocoa, sugar, and salt in a large bowl and rub in the butter until the mixture resembles breadcrumbs. Add the egg and a little cold water to form a dough. Wrap the dough and let chill in the refrigerator for 30 minutes.

Remove the pie dough from the refrigerator and roll out. Use to line ten 4-inch/10-cm tart pans. Freeze for 30 minutes. Preheat the oven to 350°F/180°C. Bake the pastry shells in the oven for 15–20 minutes. Let cool.

Place the blueberries, cassis, and confectioners' sugar in a pan and warm through so that the berries become shiny but do not burst. Let cool.

To make the filling, melt the chocolate in a heatproof bowl set over a pan of simmering water, then let cool slightly. Whip the cream until stiff and fold in the sour cream and melted chocolate.

Transfer the pastry shells to a serving plate and divide the chocolate filling among them, smoothing the surface with a spatula, then top with the blueberries.

makes 12

1 cup butter, plus extra
for greasing

1 cup brown sugar

6 fresh apricots, halved and
pitted

1 cup all-purpose flour

pinch of salt

1 tbsp superfine sugar

1 egg yolk

1 tbsp cold water

for the chocolate sauce

4 oz/115 g semisweet
chocolate

2 tbsp butter

individual apricot tartes tatin

Preheat the oven to 400°F/200°C. To make the sauce, melt the chocolate and butter together in a heatproof bowl set over a pan of gently simmering water and whisk until smooth. Set aside.

Grease a 12-hole muffin pan with butter, then line each hole with a disk of waxed paper.

Beat half of the butter with the brown sugar until very soft and divide among the holes. Place an apricot half, cut-side up, in each.

To make the pastry, place the flour and salt in a large bowl and rub in the remaining butter until the mixture resembles breadcrumbs. Stir in the superfine sugar. Add the egg yolk and a little cold water, if needed, to make a dough. Knead lightly and roll out. Cut out twelve 3-inch/7.5-cm disks and fit them over the apricot halves.

Bake for 15–20 minutes, until crisp and golden. Remove from the oven and let stand for 5 minutes. Turn out, with the apricot on top, and drizzle with the chocolate sauce to serve.

makes 16

for the pie dough

3 cups all-purpose flour, plus extra for dusting

4 tbsp shortening

4 tbsp unsalted butter

1/2 cup water

1 egg yolk, beaten, for glazing

for the filling

2 large bananas, peeled

1/2 cup finely chopped dried apricots

pinch of nutmeg

dash of orange juice

confectioners' sugar, for dusting

cream or ice cream, to serve

banana pastries

To make the pie dough, sift the flour into a large bowl. Add the shortening and butter and rub into the flour with your fingertips until the mixture resembles breadcrumbs. Gradually blend in the water to form a soft dough. Wrap in plastic wrap and let chill in the refrigerator for 30 minutes.

Preheat the oven to 350°F/180°C. Mash the bananas in a bowl with a fork and stir in the apricots, nutmeg, and orange juice, mixing well.

Roll the dough out on a lightly floured counter and cut out 16 circles, each 4 inches/10 cm in diameter.

Spoon a little of the banana filling onto one half of each circle and fold the dough over the filling to make semicircles. Pinch the edges together and seal by pressing with the prongs of a fork. Arrange the pastries on a nonstick cookie sheet and brush them with the beaten egg yolk. Cut a small slit in each pastry and bake in the preheated oven for 25 minutes, or until golden brown and crisp. Dust the banana pastries with confectioners' sugar and serve hot with cream or ice cream.

makes 12

for the pie dough

1/2 cup butter, cut into pieces,
plus extra for greasing

1¹/2 cups all-purpose flour,
plus extra for dusting

pinch of salt

2 tsp poppy seeds

cold water

for the filling

36 cherry tomatoes

1 tbsp olive oil

2 tbsp butter

2 tbsp all-purpose flour

1 cup milk

salt and pepper

1³/4 oz/50 g sharp Cheddar
cheese, grated

scant 1/2 cup cream cheese

12 fresh basil leaves

cherry tomato & poppy seed tartlets

Lightly grease a 3-inch/7.5-cm, 12-hole muffin pan. Sift the flour and salt into a food processor, add the butter, and process until the mixture resembles fine breadcrumbs. Tip the mixture into a large bowl and add the poppy seeds and a little cold water, just enough to bring the dough together. Turn out onto a floured counter and cut the dough in half. Roll out the first piece and cut out six 3¹/2-inch/9-cm circles. Take each circle and roll out to 4¹/2 inches/12 cm in diameter and fit into the muffin holes, pressing to fill the holes. Do the same with the remaining dough. Put a piece of parchment paper in each hole and fill with dried beans, then put the pan in the refrigerator to chill for 30 minutes. Meanwhile, preheat the oven to 400°F/200°C.

Remove the muffin pan from the refrigerator and bake the tartlets blind for 10 minutes in the preheated oven, then remove the paper and beans. Put the tomatoes in an ovenproof dish, drizzle with the olive oil, and roast for 5 minutes.

Melt the butter in a pan, stir in the flour, and cook for 5–8 minutes. Gradually add the milk, stirring to combine into a white sauce. Cook for an additional 5 minutes. Season well with salt and pepper and stir in the cheeses until well combined. Divide the cheese sauce among the tart shells and top with the cherry tomatoes, then put back into the oven for 15 minutes. Remove from the oven and top each tartlet with a basil leaf.

makes 6

for the pie dough

5 tbsp butter, cut into pieces, plus extra for greasing

3/4 cup all-purpose flour, plus extra for dusting

pinch of salt

cold water

for the filling

1/2 cup sour cream

1 tsp creamed horseradish

1/2 tsp lemon juice

1 tsp Spanish capers, chopped

salt and pepper

3 egg yolks

7 oz/200 g smoked salmon trimmings

bunch of fresh dill, chopped, plus extra sprigs to garnish

smoked salmon, dill & horseradish tartlets

Grease six 3½-inch/9-cm loose-bottom fluted tart pans. Sift the flour and salt into a food processor, add the butter, and process until the mixture resembles fine breadcrumbs. Tip the mixture into a large bowl and add a little cold water, just enough to bring the dough together. Turn out onto a floured counter and divide into 6 equal-size pieces. Roll each piece to fit the tart pans. Carefully fit each piece of dough in its shell and press well to fit the pan. Roll the rolling pin over the pan to neaten the edges and trim the excess dough. Cut 6 pieces of parchment paper and fit a piece into each tart, fill with dried beans, and let chill in the refrigerator for 30 minutes. Meanwhile, preheat the oven to 400°F/200°C.

Bake the tart shells for 10 minutes in the preheated oven, then remove the beans and parchment paper.

Meanwhile, put the sour cream, horseradish, lemon juice, capers, and salt and pepper into a bowl and mix well. Add the egg yolks, smoked salmon, and the dill and carefully mix again. Divide this mixture among the tart shells and return to the oven for 10 minutes. Cool in the pans for 5 minutes before serving, garnished with sprigs of dill.